NORWOOD HOUSE  PRESS

By Kathleen Corrigan

Search for Sounds
Short vowel: e

Scan this code to access the Teacher's Notes for this series or visit
www.norwoodhousepress.com/decodables

DEAR CAREGIVER, *The Decodables* series contains books following a systematic, cumulative phonics scope and sequence aligned with the science of reading. Each book in the *Search for Sounds* series allows its reader to apply their phonemic awareness and phonics knowledge in engaging and relatable texts. The keywords within each text have been carefully selected to allow readers to identify pictures beginning with sounds and letters they have been explicitly taught.

When reading these books with your child, encourage them to isolate the beginning sound in the keywords, find the corresponding picture, and identify the letter that makes the beginning sound by pointing to the letter placed in the corner of each page. Rereading the texts multiple times will allow your child the opportunity to build their letter sound fluency, a skill necessary for decoding.

You can be confident you are providing your child with opportunities to build their foundational decoding abilities which will encourage their independence as they become lifelong readers.

Happy Reading!

Emily Nudds, M.S. Ed Literacy
Literacy Consultant

e

2

MUSEUM

3

BAT CAVE

e

6

NORTH AMERICAN FOREST

ELM TREE

EVERGREENS

e

HOW TO USE THIS BOOK

Read this text with your child as they engage with each page. Then, read each keyword and ask them to isolate the beginning sound before finding the corresponding picture in the illustration. Encourage finding and pointing to the corresponding letter in the corner of the page. Additional reinforcement activities can be found in the Teacher's Notes.

Enchanting Nature
e

Pages 2 and 3	The kids had arrived! They were on a class trip to the Nature Museum. Everyone exited the bus. They were very excited.
	Inside the museum entrance was a place for kids to hang up their coats and lunch boxes. Then they walked over to the escalator. Up they went to the museum exhibits! The exhibits used models, statues, and drawings to teach people about nature.

Keywords: entrance, excited, exited, men

e

Pages 4 and 5	The first room was the Africa Room. The children saw so many interesting animals. The biggest animal of all was the elephant. The elephant model was in the middle of the room. The children learned that African elephants are the biggest land mammals on Earth today. They flap their ears to cool themselves. Their ears are just like fans. Elephants like to live together. They all look after the babies. Elephants eat grass, fruit, leaves, twigs, and tree bark. Their legs are so big and strong. The children decided the elephant was bigger than ten children!
	After they looked at the elephant, lions, and other amazing animals, they went out the exit and into the North America Room.

Keywords: elephant, exit, legs, ten

Pages 6 and 7

The North America Room had some big animals, too. The grizzly bears were very tall and the bison were amazing. But some of the children liked the elk the best.

Elk are members of the deer family but they are bigger than deer. They eat grasses in the summer and woody plants, like cedar twigs, in the winter.

Ed was so amazed by the elk that he didn't look where he was walking. He bumped into Zara and fell right by the elk's neck.

The children then left the North America Room and entered the Bat Cave. They walked under all the pretend bats hanging from the roof of the cave. Some children did not like the Bat Cave and they grabbed their teachers' elbows or hands. The bat squeaks made echoes all around them. The class walked through the Bat Cave to the exit at the other end.

Keywords: Ed, elbows, elk, exhibit, exit, fell, neck

Read this text with your child as they engage with each page. Then, read each keyword and ask them to isolate the beginning sound before finding the corresponding picture in the illustration. Encourage finding and pointing to the corresponding letter in the corner of the page. Additional reinforcement activities can be found in the Teacher's Notes.

e
Pages 8 and 9   The next room was very huge. It showed many kinds of forests. First the children looked at trees you could find in the United States, like oak trees, elm trees, and many kinds of evergreens. There were little animals hiding in the trees, too. It was fun to look for squirrels, porcupines, and birds. Then they saw amazing trees from the wet South American rainforest. They were so tall and green! They found animals in those trees, too, like an emerald tree boa and an umbrellabird.
Keywords: elm, emerald (tree boa), evergreen, vest

Pages 10 and 11

The next room made everyone laugh. It was an egg room. The displays showed that many animals hatch from eggs. There were reptile eggs, like alligator and iguana. There were insect eggs, like ant and bee. There were bird eggs, like tiny hummingbird eggs, chicken eggs, and even a giant ostrich egg.

In one corner, the museum people set up a pretend egg. It wasn't an egg. It was an eggplant. An eggplant is the fruit of a plant and it doesn't have a yolk. The children laughed when they saw the eggplant.

Then their teacher told them it was time to get on the elevator and go to eat lunch. After lunch, they would be able to see some other eggs, as well as some amazing bones. They would be going to the dinosaur exhibit. Everyone was excited! What a wonderful day!

Keywords: egg, eggplant, elevator, escalator, excited, exhibit

Norwood House Press • www.norwoodhousepress.com
The Decodables ©2024 by Norwood House Press. All Rights Reserved.
Printed in the United States of America.
367N—082023

Library of Congress Cataloging-in-Publication Data has been filed and is available at catalog.loc.gov

Literacy Consultant: Emily Nudds, M.S.Ed Literacy
Editorial and Production Development and Management: Focus Strategic Communications Inc.
Editors: Christine Gaba, Christi Davis-Martell
Illustration Credit: Mindmax
Covers: Shutterstock, Macrovector

Hardcover ISBN: 978-1-68450-719-1   Paperback ISBN: 978-1-68404-867-0
eBook ISBN: 978-1-68404-926-4